# competing in KARATE

### By RUSSELL KOZUKI

*Photographs by the author*

 STERLING PUBLISHING CO., INC. NEW YORK

 Oak Tree Press Co., Ltd. London & Sydney

## OTHER BOOKS OF INTEREST

Body-Building and Self-Defense
Complete Book of Karate
    and Self-Defense
Judo

Junior Judo
Junior Karate
Karate: Basic Principles
Karate for Young People

The author and publishers wish to thank the following for posing as models in this book: Robert Gato, Imogene Neogra, Anthony Sabato, Arthur Sibbio, and Dawn Supinski.

Third Printing, 1975

Copyright © 1974 by Sterling Publishing Co., Inc.
419 Park Avenue South, New York, N.Y. 10016
Distributed in Australia and New Zealand by Oak Tree Press Co., Ltd.,
P.O. Box J34, Brickfield Hill, Sydney 2000, N.S.W.
Distributed in the United Kingdom and elsewhere in the British Commonwealth
by Ward Lock Ltd., 116 Baker Street, London W 1
*Manufactured in the United States of America*
*All rights reserved*
Library of Congress Catalog Card No.: 74-82337
Sterling ISBN 0-8069-4080-8 Trade         Oak Tree 7061-2025-6
                    4081-6 Library

# Contents

**Illus. 1**

# Free-Style Sparring Techniques

Free-style sparring is the combat sport of karate. It is the nearest thing to an actual fight between two unarmed opponents. It is also a test of fighting skills with built-in safeguards. All blows and kicks are stopped just short of actual contact, and strict obedience of the rules is expected of every contestant. Unsportsmanlike conduct or action that endangers the safety of your opponent can result in immediate dismissal.

Sometimes there may be a slight variance of the ground rules depending on the size, locale, the importance of the contest, and other factors. Compared to wrestling or boxing, *sport* karate is still in its infancy. Because of this, more rules changes are expected as karate's leading practitioners continue their determined efforts to promote a safer—and more exciting—sport.

Although a karate player training for free-style fighting should already have mastered most of the basic karate techniques, he still will have much to learn before he acquires the competitive proficiency of the seasoned veteran. As in other forms of athletics, there are no substitutes for hard work and sincere effort.

It is important for a trainee to use his full understanding of the basic karate principles and apply them in the highly specialized area of karate free-style sparring. No attempt is made here to include the rudiments of basic karate or its forms. Instead, the emphasis in this book is on fighting stances, proper body shifting, combination techniques, attacks, and counter-attacks designed to score against fast-moving opponents.

Basic karate techniques can be learned from my other books.

# Fighting Stances

The karateka's ability to respond effectively to different attacks depends largely upon his training, and the type of stance employed for a given situation. It would be impossible to find a single perfect stance for every type of attack or defence. To some degree, all stances have their weak and strong points though most karatekas do have their special ones. Physical characteristics such as height, weight, and speed of foot may determine the type of stance most suitable for you.

## Forward Stance

Used mostly for straight frontal attacks, the Forward Stance is very strong to the front, but lacks mobility to the side. (Demonstrated by the karateka on the left in Illus. 2.)

Illus. 2

Illus. 3—The Forward Stance is often used when strong, direct power can be advantageously employed in a final attack.

# Horse Stance

Illus. 4. The Horse Stance.

Illus. 5—This is a strong defensive stance against attacks from the side, but it is also lacking in all-round mobility.

Both the Forward and Horse Stances are low, rigid, and somewhat limited to straight-line movements, but can be extremely effective and useful in certain situations.

## Cat Stance

The Cat Stance is primarily a defensive stance which complements the use of knifehand techniques. A speedy Front Kick with the forward foot can be easily done from this position, but neither the kicks nor hand techniques will have the power of other stances, due to the narrow foot positions this stance requires. However, you are able to literally leap out of danger quickly by using both feet simultaneously to jump away. This is possible because of the narrow stance. The principal thing to remember is not to jeopardize your balance by jumping too high, or trying to cover too much ground in a single leap.

Illus. 6—Defender backs out of range of Attacker's Front Kick.

Illus. 6

## Back Stance

This stance is preferred by many free-style fighters for quick movements and ease of changing into another stance. Speedy and versatile, the Back Stance may be used either in the half-front or side-facing position.

Illus. 7—These female karatekas are using the relaxed version of the Back Stance which is used mostly in free-style sparring. Outward pressure should be kept on the slightly bent rear leg to facilitate quick movements.

# Bull Stance

Illus. 8—The entire body weight is evenly supported on both feet in the Bull Stance. For this reason, it is also called the 50–50 or the Even Stance. Its greatest advantage is all-round flexibility—a strong, stable base for both offensive and defensive moves. You can use either foot to execute kicks without first shifting your body weight drastically to the supporting leg.

Illus. 9—When in a defensive posture, your body should be turned at an angle in a half-front facing position so that you present only a limited target against your opponent.

**Illus. 8**

The distance between the heel of your forward leg and the toes of your rear foot is almost a third less than that of the more rigid Forward Stance. The resulting higher body balance is more than equated by greater flexibility and mobility. Always keep both knees slightly bent and your upper body straight.

Illus. 10

## Side Stance

The Side Stance employed in free fighting is basically a short Horse Stance. You can utilize it to good advantage when executing Side Kicks or quick Back Fist Strikes against your opponent. Also this stance provides very little opening for an opponent's possible counter-attacks when your guarding arms are kept in their proper blocking position.

Illus. 10—A fist blow is being deflected with a Fist Hammer Strike from the Side Stance.

14

# Body Shifting

Regardless of the stance used, good body posture and strong balance must be maintained to ensure the effectiveness of any given technique. Improper shifting of your body will result in poor body balance and weaken any attack or defensive effort. Correct timing of body movements is required whether moving forward, backwards, or even in a circular direction. The center of gravity should be shifted smoothly as your body moves.

It is extremely important that a karateka does not

**Illus. 11. Beginning a body-shifting drill.**

neglect this phase of karate training. Much practice is needed, of course, but eventually you will develop good body balance along with the ability to execute your techniques far more effectively.

Innumerable technique combinations are possible for body-shifting drills. A good example of this type of

Illus. 12. A Palm Heel Thrust leading into a . . .

drill is the Palm Heel Thrust, Front Kick, Side Kick, Roundhouse Kick, and Overhead Back Fist Strike as shown in Illus. 11, 12, 13, 14, 15 and 16. Remember always to finish up in the on-guard position. You can practice these drills alone as well as with a partner.

Illus. 13. . . . Front Kick, followed by a . . .

Illus. 14. . . . Side Kick.

Illus. 15. Then the attacker delivers a Roundhouse Kick . . .

Illus. 16. . . . and finishes the body-shifting drill with an Overhead Back Fist Strike.

# Space Intervals

Space interval is that critical distance, or measureable space, between two opponents. During free-sparring encounters, a karate fighter must be alert to the changes in his position as related to that of his opponent. While moving about looking for an opening, your opponent may move towards or away from you, depending on the situation. You should make certain that there is enough distance between you and your opponent so that he is forced to move forward at least half a step to adjust his space interval in order to reach you with his intended attack. In other words, he must "close in" half a step before launching his attack, or else he will be just short of effective striking range.

Let us assume that you have detected his subtle "closing-in" move. You can counter his effort by moving away while being prepared to block at the same time. The other alternative is instantly to counter-attack by moving in against him. This method of "beating him to the punch" often catches the attacker by surprise because he finds himself moving in the wrong direction.

There are times when the defender may find it impossible to move quickly out of range. Then he must depend on his blocking techniques to deflect his opponent's kicks or punches until he can counter-attack. In such situations, the blocks are most effective when executed with body shifting and movement.

Illus. 17 and 18—The opponents are at a dangerous fighting distance. Their space interval is incorrect since either one can be easily struck by the other without the attacker ever having to move his feet. Always maintain enough distance from your opponent so that his kicks or blows fail to reach the target unless he moves his foot and body forward before he executes his attacking technique.

It does not matter whether you are attacking or defending. The basic principle of space interval remains the same. Keep the proper distance between yourself and your opponent at all times. When he attempts to close in, you should move away the same distance, *or* suddenly counter-attack.

Illus. 19, 20, and 21 demonstrate the importance of making necessary distance adjustments against the closing-in efforts of the attacker.

**Illus. 19**

Illus. 20

Illus. 21. Here the defender alertly makes the move in time to avoid being struck by the blow.

# Closing In

There are four basic methods of closing in or making distance adjustments in order to move within effective striking range of your opponent.

## Method #1

This method can be used as a closing-in effort, or to launch a sudden counter-attack. Move your forward foot half a step to the front while bringing up your rear foot the same distance. You should now be in attacking distance unless your opponent has detected your attempt

Illus. 22. Preparing to close in.

**Illus. 23**

and prudently moved away. However, the same type of technique can be applied if the situation is reversed.

Illus. 22, 23, 24, 25—Suppose your opponent is about to move in. Instead of retreating, suddenly advance your front foot half a step, thrusting your body forward with the rear leg and executing the Lunge Punch to the opponent's face at the same time. Follow through with a Front Kick to his body.

Illus. 24. A Lunge Punch, followed by a . . .

Illus. 25. . . . Front Kick to the body.

## Method #2

Illus. 26, 27, and 28—In this method you bring your rear foot almost next to your forward foot. At this instant you can advance your forward foot as in Method #1, or continue advancing your rear foot past your front foot to a forward position.

The important thing to bear in mind is that the entire movement be executed in one smooth motion.

**Illus. 28**

Illus. 29

## Method #3

Stepping sideways across your own foot is a method often used to close in rapidly on your opponent, usually to deliver a Side Kick. This is best done from a Side Stance. Although considered to be a good defensive stance, it is limited in attacking techniques. Nevertheless, the Side Stance can be very useful in certain free-fighting situations. A variation of cross stepping frequently used in free-style is performed simply by bringing one leg sideways next to the other.

Illus. 29, 30, and 31 show how cross stepping is done.

Illus. 30. Closing in with the cross step.

Illus. 31. Ending the cross step with a Side Kick.

# Method #4

Sometimes you can pursue and close in on your opponent by utilizing the forward momentum produced during the attack. An excellent example of this is the Hopping Front Kick.

To execute this technique, cock your rear foot to kicking position, and hop strongly forward on your supporting leg. At the same time, deliver a thrusting Front Kick to the opponent's body.

This technique is doubly effective when a conventional Front Kick (Illus. 33) precedes the Hopping Kick.

**Illus. 32**

Illus. 35. The Hopping Front Kick is delivered.

# Versatility

Every karateka should strive to be effective with his techniques from his left side as well as his right. Your opponent will be much more difficult to cope with if he discovers that you are effective only on one side.

When executing the Front Kick, be sure to use the foot which gives you the best opportunity to score.

Let's presume that both you and your opponent have your left leg in the forward position, and he suddenly moves in by advancing his front leg. You may wish to counter with a quick Front Kick to his body. Normally, you might prefer to use your rear leg for greater kicking power, but in this instance it would be difficult to get your kick past his left guard arm which is on the same side as his advancing leg. Therefore, a fast Front Kick with your forward leg would have far greater chance of success.

Illus. 36 and 37 show defender counter-attacking with his front foot just as attacker moves in, but in Illus. 38 and 39, the charging attacker is stopped by a strong Front Kick delivered with the rear foot.

Illus. 36. Attacker, on left, moves in.

Illus. 37. Defender counter-attacks with his front foot.

**Illus. 38. Here the attacker, on right, charges in.**

Illus. 39. Defender stops attacker with a Front Kick with his rear leg.

# Concentration

As the free-style trainee makes progress in his free-fighting techniques, he is invariably confronted with the problem of where to look with his eyes.

There are those who strongly advocate looking directly into your opponent's eyes for signs of his intentions, or a hint of impending movement. However, there is another school of thought which conflicts with this theory.

Fixing your eyes on any given spot may also fix your mind to a single spot, and inadvertently lead to neglect of other areas. Thus it is presumed better to look at your opponent's face, focusing more or less on his eyes. Actually you should look at him as a whole person—that is, from head to foot. If you are too intent on watching only certain areas, you will be in danger of being misled by your opponent's fake moves.

Later, at the advanced stages of karate proficiency, the veteran karateka can actually sense the intended attack and move even before his opponent does. Of course, such a high degree of skill is not easily achieved without training your mind as well as your body.

In free-style sparring, the karateka must not permit his mind to dwell on such thoughts as the possible superiority of his opponent, but try to maintain a calm, open mind so that he is able instantly to respond to his opponent's attack.

# Combination Techniques

Scoring against an alert opponent with a single kick or blow may prove very difficult, especially if he works from a tight defensive posture. In such situations, it is best to attack with different technique combinations.

The purpose of these attacks is to take advantage of the possible disturbed body posture of an opponent after your initial attack. Often the second or the third technique will score where ordinarily a single attack might be blocked and effectively countered.

Any number of combinations, fakes, and counter-moves are possible from the vast karate repertoire. Presented here are some of the most practical and frequently used free-fighting moves.

## Deflecting, or Grabbing, Technique

Illus. 40, 41, 42, and 43—Slide forward with your advanced foot to adjust the space interval against your opponent. While trying to close in, deflect, or grab, his guard arm to distract him. Execute a Front Kick with your rear foot. Follow through with a Reverse Punch to the face and a Lunge Punch to the body.

Illus. 40

Illus. 42. As you grab his guard arm, deliver a Front Kick.

Illus. 43. Follow with a Reverse Punch to his face and a Lunge Punch to his body.

# Side Kick, Roundhouse Kick, Back Kick

Illus. 44, 45, 46, 47, and 48—If you are facing your opponent with your side turned towards him, close in by using the cross-stepping procedure, and deliver a Side Kick to the body. Should your opponent evade the kick, follow up with a Roundhouse Kick to the neck. Continue the rotating movement of your body, and place your kicking foot on the ground a little to his side. Be careful to protect your exposed back with your guard arm as you turn. Complete your pivot, and execute a Back Kick with your other foot.

**Illus. 44**

Illus. 45. If your Side Kick fails . . .

Illus. 46. . . . try a Roundhouse Kick with the other leg.

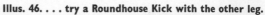

Illus. 47. Be sure that you protect your back with your guard arm when you pivot.

**Illus. 48. After you have completed pivoting, deliver a Back Kick with the other foot.**

**Illus. 49**

## Double Front Kick

Illus. 49, 50, 51, and 52—This type of technique often works against an opponent who prefers not to move very much while on the defensive. After adjusting for proper attacking distance, execute two Front Kicks in rapid-fire fashion to your opponent's body. Deliver both kicks with your rear foot, one after the other, as your entire body moves forward.

Illus. 50. Closing in.

Illus. 51. First, kick with one foot.

Illus. 52. Then deliver the second kick as quickly as you can with the other foot. Follow through with a Lunge Punch to the face.

# Leaping Double Back Fist

Illus. 53, 54, and 55—First correct your space interval by closing in on your opponent. Jump up on your forward foot, directing a Back Fist Strike to his head while bringing the knee of the other leg up to protect your groin area. This is the leg you pivot on when you land.

Rotate your body in mid-air so that you can execute a Back Fist Strike with your opposite fist at the end of the turning movement as your foot touches the ground.

**Illus. 53. Closing in.**

Illus. 54. As you jump up on one foot, raise your other knee high to protect yourself.

Illus. 55. Back up your Back Fist Strike with a Snap Side Kick to the body.

# Low Flying Front Kick

Illus. 56, 57, 58, 59, and 60—High jump or flying kicks are primarily weapons of surprise. It is not easy to score against an alert opponent with this type of technique unless his body posture and balance have been first disturbed by other preceding attacks. This same rule also applies to the Low Flying Front Kick, except that its detection by an opponent is a bit more difficult, and there is far less danger involved should the kick be blocked.

Illus. 56. Closing in.

**Illus. 57. First, deliver a Front Kick.**

This will often work on an opponent who does not expect a second long-range kicking effort, and is unprepared to move quickly enough to avoid the attack.

After adjusting for attacking distance, execute a Front Kick with your rear leg. Continue forward momentum, landing and jumping up to deliver another front kick with the same leg. Simultaneously bring up the knee of your other leg to protect the groin area and to assist in adding impetus to the jumping kick.

Illus. 58. Withdraw your kicking leg.

Illus. 59. Jump up high preparatory to delivering another kick with the same leg.

**Illus. 60. Delivering the Low Flying Front Kick.**

# Front Kick, Lunge Punch, Reverse Punch

Illus. 61, 62, 63, and 64—An opportune moment for a quick Front Kick with your rear leg may present itself when you catch your opponent just as he moves in.

Follow through with a Lunge Punch to his face and a Reverse Punch to his body.

Illus. 61. Attacker, on left, moves in.

Illus. 62. A quick Front Kick is delivered by the defender.

Illus. 63. Now the defender quickly executes a Lunge Punch to his opponent's face.

Illus. 64. Finally, a Reverse Punch to the body.

# Fakes

Even your best techniques will often fail unless you first employ fake moves to disturb your opponent's body posture and balance. He will leave an opening in his defences if he over-reacts to your false moves. At that very instant you have a fleeting opportunity to score with your technique before he recovers.

## Palm Heel Strike

Illus. 65, 66, and 67—Close in to correct attacking distance, and suddenly thrust your palm heel to your opponent's face. This will cause him to bring up his blocking arm to protect his face. If possible, grab his sleeve as he attempts the blocking motion, and execute a Reverse Punch to the body.

**Illus. 65**

Illus. 66. Grasp your opponent's sleeve if you can as he tries to block your Palm Heel Strike.

**Illus. 67. Immediately after you deliver your Reverse Punch, follow up with a Front Kick.**

# Overhead Fist Hammer Strike

Illus. 68, 69, 70, and 71—If your opponent backs away despite your efforts to close in, quickly leap forward with a fake Overhead Fist Hammer Strike to his face, forcing him to attempt an Overhead Block. Turn your body so that you will land sideways to him. Protect your back with your guard arm against a possible fist blow while turning, and strongly execute a Wheel Kick to his body.

Normally you would not charge in after your opponent. However, since he is moving in the wrong direction, the chances of an effective instant counter are minimal.

**Illus. 68**

Illus. 69. The Fake Overhead Fist Hammer Strike compels your opponent to react with a block.

Illus. 70. As you turn, be sure to protect your back.

Illus. 71. The Fake Fist Hammer Strike worked! Here, a quick, powerful Wheel Kick reaches its target.

# Knifehand Strike, Reverse Punch

Illus. 72, 73, 74, and 75—When two evenly matched opponents are cautiously adjusting and counter-adjusting the space intervals between them, a sudden, swift attack sometimes can tip the scales to the side of the attacker.

If you are in a left-foot forward position, execute the Overhead Knifehand Strike with your right hand while raising your right leg to protect your groin area. Place your right foot in the right-foot forward position, and deliver a left Reverse Punch to the body at almost the

**Illus. 72. Adjusting the space interval.**

Illus. 73. An unexpected Overhead Knifehand Strike.

same time. This will force your opponent to block strongly to deflect your punch. Execute a quick Lunge Punch to his exposed face with your right hand.

Illus. 74. A quick left Reverse Punch, followed by . . .

Illus. 75. . . . a Lunge Punch to his face.

# Fist Hammer Strike to the Face

Illus. 76, 77, and 78—This is a variation of the Fist Hammer Strike discussed on page 68. The technique is useful against opponents who constantly change their forward foot position as you adjust your attacking distance. Move in strongly with a Fist Hammer Strike to your opponent's face from your protected side to force him to use a High Block to guard his face. Deliver a Front Snap Kick to his exposed armpit.

**Illus. 76. Adjusting the space interval.**

Illus. 77. The Fist Hammer Strike.

Illus. 78. The Front Snap Kick follows the Fist Hammer Strike.

## Side Kick to the Body

Illus. 79, 80, 81, and 82—A fake Side Kick can sometimes be used as a second closing-in effort just as your opponent steps away from your first attempt. Close in from the Side Stance, and deliver the fake Side Kick to the body. Step forward with your kicking foot into a Bull Stance and follow through with a Front Kick to his mid-section, using your rear foot to execute the kick.

**Illus. 79. If your first closing in fails, try again from a Side Stance.**

Illus. 80. Closing in from the Side Stance.

Illus. 81. The fake Side Kick.

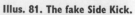

Illus. 81. The fake Side Kick.

Illus. 82. Follow up with the Front Kick.

**Illus. 83**

## Low Fake Kick

Illus. 83, 84, 85, and 86—This kick is usually directed at the thigh area and knee. It can be employed against an opponent who habitually moves just out of reach without making any real effort to block with his hands, which he prefers to keep ready for a fast counter-attack.

If in a left-foot Forward, Side, or Back Stance, close in by bringing up your rear foot next to your front foot, and execute a Side Kick to the lower half of your opponent's body. Then place your kicking foot on the ground a little to the side of him.

Illus. 84. Closing in to deliver a Low Fake Kick.

Illus. 85. A fake Side Kick is delivered. Quickly place your kicking foot on the ground and start to pivot on it.

Illus. 86. Be careful to protect your back as you rotate your body to execute a Wheel or Hook Kick to your opponent's body.

Illus. 87. Closing in from a Front Thrust Kick.

Illus. 88. Preparing to deliver the fake kick.

# Front Thrust Kick

Illus. 87, 88, 89, and 90—The forward drive of the Front Thrust Kick is frequently employed to correct space intervals so that the attacker will be within the effective attacking range when he executes his technique.

Follow up the fake kick with another Front Kick by placing the fake kicking leg on the ground, and kicking the opponent's body with the rear foot.

**Illus. 89. The fake Front Kick.**

Illus. 90. The fake Front Thrust Kick is followed by another Front Kick that reaches its target.

# Fake Back Fist to the Head

Illus. 91, 92, 93, and 94—As your opponent moves in to adjust his attacking distance, withdraw your front leg so that you are facing him in either a Bull Stance or Back Stance. Use your fake Back Fist to draw his blocking arm up, and execute a kick to his body with your front foot. Follow through with a Lunge Punch.

Illus. 91

Illus. 92. The fake Back Fist . . .

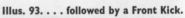

Illus. 93. . . . followed by a Front Kick.

Illus. 94. Finally, a Lunge Punch.

# Counter-Attacking Techniques

There is a saying in karate that one should be attacking while defending. To put it another way, you must attack at the same instant you block your opponent's kicks or blows. This type of instant response makes it extremely difficult for your opponent to execute his combination or follow-up techniques. Instead, he is forced to go on the defensive, thereby losing the initiative.

Points are often scored in free-style matches when the attacking karateka fails to react quickly to his opponent's successful block and counter-attack.

## Knee Block and Reverse Punch Counter

Illus. 95, 96, and 97—This is a simple, but effective defence against a front kick when used just as your opponent begins his kicking attempt. Bring up the knee of your forward leg to jam his kick, thrusting your body slightly to the side and execute a Reverse Punch to the face.

Illus. 95. The opponent (on left) is about to deliver a kick with his right foot.

Illus. 96. The Knee Block thwarts the Front Kick of the opponent.

**Illus. 97. The Reverse Punch.**

# Side Kick Counter

Illus. 98, 99, 100—Just as your opponent moves into kicking position, strike quickly at his foreleg with a Low Side Kick. This will make it impossible for him to complete his kick without first regaining his body balance and posture. Place your blocking leg on the ground, and counter with a fast Front Kick to the body.

**Illus. 98**

Illus. 99. The Low Side Kick.

Illus. 100. The Front Kick.

## Crescent Kick Block, Side Kick Counter

Illus. 101, 102, and 103—When used as a block, the sweeping arc of the Crescent Kick can be most effectively utilized from the Back Stance since most of your body weight is already on your rear leg. This permits quick movement with your front leg.

To deflect an opponent's Front Kick, sweep aside his kicking leg with the flat part of your foot. Do not place the kicking foot on the ground. Withdraw only slightly to cock into kicking position, and drive a thrusting Side Kick to the body.

Illus. 101

**Illus. 102. The Crescent Kick block.**

Illus. 103. The Side Kick.

# Scoop Block, Back Fist Counter

Illus. 104 and 105—A determined opponent with a strong Front Kick can be very difficult to stop, but side-stepping in a circular movement while employing the underhand Scoop Block against his kick will enable you to avoid the full power of his frontal attack. The technique must be executed smoothly as if one movement. Counter with two quick Back Fist Strikes to the groin and face.

**Illus. 104. The Scoop Block.**

**Illus. 105. The Back Fist Counter.**

# Crescent Kick Counter

Illus. 106, 107, 108, and 109—Block or deflect the opponent's attack with a Back Fist Strike while dropping back into a Side Stance. Counter-attack by driving a Crescent Kick to the body. The supporting leg should be pointed straight ahead at the completion of the kick. Follow through with an Elbow Strike to face and body.

**Illus. 106**

Illus. 107. Blocking with a Back Fist Strike.

Illus. 108. Crescent Kick to the body.

Illus. 109. Elbow Strike.

## Double Arm Block, Back Fist Counter

The principle involved in this technique is jamming the opponent's Roundhouse Kick by moving in close against him.

Step in with your lead foot, and execute a Double Knifehand Block on his kicking leg. Counter with a Back Fist to his face, using the fist nearest to him. In the same motion, spin in a tight pivot towards your back, and execute another Back Fist Strike with the other hand.

**Illus. 110. The Double Arm Block.**

Illus. 111. The Back Fist Counter . . .

Illus. 112. . . . followed by another Back Fist with the other hand.

## Wheel Kick Counter

Speedy and effective, the Wheel Kick can be used to a good advantage against an opponent who relies mostly on hand techniques. If he moves in fast, cross-step quickly to avoid his charge. Protect your back while making the pivot. Execute the Wheel or Hook Kick to his body. However, should your opponent attempt to close in slowly, disturb his posture and balance with a fake kick aimed at his body. Continue your rotating motion to deliver the Wheel Kick. Follow through with a Back Fist Strike to the face (Illus. 116).

**Illus. 113. The fake kick.**

Illus. 114. Making the pivot.

Illus. 115. Delivering the Wheel Kick.

**Illus. 116. Finally, a Back Fist Strike to the face.**

# Index